CAROL STREAM PUBLIC LIBRARY

3 1319 00495 5412

W9-BRE-427

To my mother, Gerri, for her endless love

JANETTA OTTER-BARRY BOOKS

*Eye on the Wild: Gorilla* copyright © Frances Lincoln Limited 2012
Text and photographs copyright © Suzi Eszterhas 2012

The right of Suzi Eszterhas to be identified as the author and photographer of this work
has been asserted by her in accordance with the Copyright, Designs and Patents Act,
1988 (United Kingdom).

First published in Great Britain and in the USA in 2012 by
Frances Lincoln Children's Books, 4 Torriano Mews,
Torriano Avenue, London NW5 2RZ
www.franceslincoln.com

All rights reserved

No part of this publication may be reproduced, stored in a retrieval system, or transmitted,
in any form, or by any means, electrical, mechanical, photocopying, recording or otherwise
without the prior written permission of the publisher or a licence permitting restricted
copying. In the United Kingdom such licences are issued by the Copyright Licensing Agency,
Saffron House, 6-10 Kirby Street, London EC1N 8TS.

A catalogue record for this book is available from the British Library.

ISBN 978-1-84780-299-6

Set in Stempel Schneidler

Printed in Dongguan, Guangdong, China by Toppan Leefung in November 2011

1 3 5 7 9 8 6 4 2

# GORILLA

## Suzi Eszterhas

**F**

FRANCES LINCOLN
CHILDREN'S BOOKS

Carol Stream Public Library
Carol Stream, Illinois 60188-1634

J.
599.884
ESZ

Far away, in the misty moutains of Africa, a baby gorilla is born. The tiny bundle of black fur needs to be looked after just like a human baby. Mom is with her all the time, holding the baby close to her big chest and keeping her warm and safe.

8/12

The baby gorilla has a big family, including Mom and Dad, brothers and sisters, uncles, aunts and cousins. Sometimes there can be as many as 30 gorillas living in one, big, family group.

The baby gorilla's father is called a silverback,
because of the silver-colored hair on his back.
The silverback is the boss. He has the very important
job of leading and protecting the whole family.

The gorilla mom loves her baby very much. She holds her all the time and gives her lots of hugs and kisses. For six whole years Mom takes care of her baby and teaches her how to live in the jungle.

The baby gorilla spends her first few months constantly in her mother's arms. She has to use her tiny fingers to cling to Mom's long hair, otherwise she might fall off. She is very sleepy and Mom's arms make a perfect place to take a nap.

**W**hen the baby gorilla is three months old, she can sit up, crawl – and smile – just like a human baby. Sometimes, she even sucks her thumb!

The hungry little gorilla drinks
Mom's milk many times every day
for three years. This milk will help her
to grow big and strong.

The baby gorilla learns by watching and copying her mother. Sitting on Mom's head gives her a great view and is good fun, too. Meanwhile, Mom shows her which plants taste good and which taste bad.

By her first birthday, the baby gorilla is starting to explore her jungle home. She is a little more steady on her feet now and loves to climb bamboo and vines. Mom lets her explore and play, but she is always close by – and watching carefully – in case she has to rush in to the rescue.

One of the baby gorilla's favorite games is piggyback riding, cruising around on Mom's back. Mom doesn't have a stroller, of course, so when her baby grows too big and heavy to carry in her arms, she gives her a piggyback ride. It's safe, and Mom can still move easily through the thick jungle.

Gorillas groom each other a lot, and Mom likes to keep her baby very clean. She uses her fingers to pick bugs and dirt out of the baby's fur. One day the baby will know how to groom herself and other gorillas.

When the baby gorilla is three years old, she is bursting with energy and loves to wrestle with her brothers, sisters, and cousins. Playtime helps her to get to know all the other members of the big family. It might look scary – but it's just good fun.

**A**t the age of four, the young gorilla knows all the best plants to eat and how to eat them. She eats roots, shoots, fruit, wild celery, vines, tree bark, and even stinging nettles.

Gorillas talk to each other all the time. They make lots of weird and wonderful sounds and also pull faces. The young gorilla has to learn to say things by grunting, belching, screaming, barking, and roaring!

On her sixth birthday, the young gorilla is grown up. All this time she has learned how to be a good mother by quietly watching her own mother and all the other gorilla moms in her family. Now she is ready to have a baby of her own!

# More about Gorillas

- Gorilla babies weigh only four pounds when they are born. But by the time they are grown up, they weigh up to 500 pounds (over 100 times the size they were born).

- Gorillas eat all day long. They eat over 100 different plants and have huge bellies that can hold up to 40 pounds of food a day!

- Gorillas use their hands as feet when they walk. This is called knuckle-walking.

- Gorillas make many different sounds. They belch when they are happy and cough, scream or beat their chests when they are upset.

- Silverback male gorillas weigh twice as much as gorilla moms and are bigger than even the biggest football players!

- Gorillas break branches and leaves to make nests to sleep in at the top of trees. They do not sleep in the same nest for more than one night, so they make a new nest every night.

- Gorillas live in the tropical and subtropical forests of Africa, along the equator. They are endangered because people are destroying the jungles they live in and poaching them.

- Find out more on www.gorillafund.org